AF582892

Hello there, my name is Charlie and also I am mosting likely to inform you a tale of exactly how my friend, Sanford, saved Christmas.

Sanford is a dog. Actually, he's a pooch. He is mixed with Laboratory, Collie, German shepherd, and reported to be part Cocker Spaniel. He's big! I assume he considers at least a hundred pounds, yet do not allow his amplitude trouble you. He was a softy, 100%!

So as you can see he is not your ordinary pet dog. He is a black and also brownish speckled pet with some splotches of white patches. He likewise uses a cape.

When he first began wearing the cape I assumed it was a negative idea. I mean, the number of canines do you recognize wear a cape? He told me he was using it to safeguard his secret identity.

Sanford and I live in a secret city in Southern California. We have a private detective agency which is also in a secret place in an alley behind a dumpster. To obtain entrance to our workplace you have actually reached knock one-time and also ring the doorbell twice.

By the way, I'm a mouse. Currently, do not shriek! That isn't essential. I am a great computer mouse. I normally ride on Sanford's back.

Someday, we were consuming some donuts. I stated, "Sanford, what are we going to do? We haven't had a client in weeks."

He licked some jelly off his paw and also said, "Do not fret Charlie. I sense

something exceptional will show up."
It was remarkable when I consider it.

Equally as he said it there was a loud crashing noise. It appeared as though something large had actually come under the dumpster. Sanford told me to take a look. He constantly made ME have a look. He said it was due to the fact that I was so small nobody would certainly see me. Yeah, well, if that were true I wouldn't have individuals trying to strike me with a mop daily.
Yet, Sanford was my manager. Whatever Sanford told me to do ... I did it. He viewed me creep out the door. I sensed he was seeing me creep up the dumpster, also. See the dumpster terrified me. The last few times I checked the dumpster I had mistakenly fallen under it and obtained stuck. Sanford had to concern obtain me. When he has to obtain me, it typically implied him sticking me in his smelly mouth and tossing me, which was not enjoyable.
I looked in wonder at what I saw. It was a huge fat reindeer! I searched for in the evening sky. I saw nothing. "Hmmmm ... What the ...".
" Charlie," Sanford stated in a murmur, "What is it?".
" It's a reindeer, Sanford," I stated. "But I do not know which one it is, or where it came from.".
" Charlie, I think you have been consuming too many donuts. There is no such thing as a reindeer." Sanford was no more whispering yet chatting noisally.

I frowned at him as well as said, "Don't chew out me!" When I recognized I was yelling at my employer I claimed louder, "SORRY!".
" It's fine. I shouldn't have yelled," Sanford said sorry to me. He strolled closer

to the dumpster which created it to tremble a little.
" Hey, hello ..." I panicked, "What are you doing?" I was trembling and also stumbling.

" I'm going to get up there and see what's within." "Oh no, you're not!" I stated back to him.
Sanford increased his paws and jumped in. Of course, as he landed I fell in also. We both landed with a thump on top of the sleeping reindeer. The reindeer discharge a gruff and irritable growl. "Arghh ..." the reindeer stated.
" I assume it's mad at us," I said to Sanford. "Leave of me," the reindeer demanded.
" Why don't you get out from under us initially?" Sanford recommended. Oh, one thing I ought to point out, Sanford always begins an argument. "Do not you recognize that I am?" the reindeer asked.
" No, we do not. This leads us to our following inquiry. Who are you?" Sanford asked.
" I'm Comet," he stated to us as he stayed up. "No you aren't," Sanford said. Comet stood in the stack of garbage and drank himself. Banana peels, plastic bags, orange peels and also various other things flew off of him as well as basically buried me deeper as well as much deeper into the heap. See, there was a misconception that mice like garbage and also unclean areas, but the reality was I couldn't stand trash. My home as well as workplace were cool and tidy. I didn't like dumpsters as well as I attempted to encourage Sanford to relocate our office on a number of events.
Comet looked into Sanford's eyes and also said firmly, "Yes, I am." Currently I was getting cranky. "Verify it smart man.".

Then he flew out of the trash bin. I'm not joking. He really flew out of the dumpster. Why could not he have placed me on his back first? Wouldn't that have been the Santa's reindeer point to do? Assist a friendly mouse out? Sanford slanted his head to his ideal side. His mouth opened up then.

closed.

" Currently what?" I asked. I was obtaining crankier. "Where would certainly he go?" Sanford asked me.
" I'm right below," we spoke with the side of the dumpster. "I shed my.

flying powers because of Sashi," Comet described. "I can only fly a couple of backyards.".

" If you can just fly a couple of backyards, how did you end up in this dumpster?" I asked as I was trying to climb up onto Sanford's back. I wanted to get safe onto him before he had the urge to place me in his mouth once more and also throw me.
" I believed I had my powers back and determined to check it out. Nevertheless, Christmas Eve is only in a few more days. Well, just when I was flying at the rate of light ... all of a sudden ... the power quit and I dropped in a spiral. I can not handle spinning or falling. I should have passed out on my means down.".
Sanford was so caught up in what Comet was claiming that he had not understood I was securely tucked into the bands of his cape. So when he lastly

leapt out of the dumpster, I was out with him.
" Well, why do not you enter into our office? We can establish a situation for you," Sanford politely welcomed.
Comet looked weary. His eyes were bloodshot. He resembled he might utilize a donut and also maybe some milk. Comet followed us right into our workplace.

He was substantial. He hardly fit through our secret door. Our door seemed it was simply a concrete wall yet. it was a door.
When we were inside I embarked on Sanford's back and mosted likely to the box of donuts. "Hey Comet, aid on your own. Oh, as well as have some milk.".
" We have milk?" Sanford asked stunned.
" Yeah, it's my secret stockpile. You aren't supposed to have any type of," I advised him. Sanford was lactose intolerant.
Comet ate two donuts in 2 attacks. His eyes seemed to glimmer after he consumed alcohol some milk. He slapped his lips.
" So to service," Sanford stated. "That's Sashi?".
Comet shivered a little, "She's an insane psycho raccoon who is trying to take over the North Post. I had attempted to advise Santa before however he really did not listen to me. Santa thinks I drink way too much Egg Nog. In some cases I do however not that day. I saw Sashi standing on a fallen log providing a speech to a few other raccoons as well as a number of other animals. She stated she stole guide of the North. She said the book had many enchanting spells, remedy dishes and also de-powering spells. Sashi stated she prepared to make Santa think the reindeer are crumbling and also can no longer fly. Santa will need to resort to other animals. When the moment pertains to deliver the

presents, who will just happen to be standing there when Santa is trying to find a choice to ride his sleigh? A lot of negative raccoons, that's that! Sashi claimed she would certainly remove Rudolph initially.".

" So what 'd she do to Rudolph?".

" Nothing. She got to me initially, by accident".

Comet made an odd face. We listened to a puff of air coming from Comet's back side after that bubbles appeared. Unexpectedly the odor of cinnamon.

went into the air as each bubble stood out. Comet took a deep, pleased breath.

"Excuse me," he claimed nicely.

" So how would certainly being able to fly the sleigh result in taking control of the North Pole?" Sanford asked.

Comet looked sad as he clarified, "They plan to press Santa out of the sleigh eventually while he is delivering toys.".

" Wow," both Sanford as well as I stated in unison.

Comet laid down as well as place his directly the carpet. "I can't do anything about it currently.".

" Oh yes we can!" Sanford stated.

I never recognized what Sanford was believing. Yet, usually when he stated we might do something, we could. When Sanford set his mind to something, watch out!

Comet looked worried as well as uncertain.

Sanford overlooked Comet's doubtfulness as well as asked, "Exactly how did Sashi make you shed your powers?".

Comet looked guiltily at both of us as he stated, "Sashi cast a spell on Rudolph's water. I was still dehydrated after I drank every one of my water so I snuck right into Rudolph's stall and also consumed his." Comet drank his head and looked down at his hooves. "I understand, it was wrong. After that my belly started to hurt. I listened to Sashi in the next delay stating the spell while all the other reindeer were sleeping. She said, "Ha ha ho ho na no no ta to pa po no more high fly in the night sk. Hocus pocus ardichokus." After that Sashi said, "I will certainly have vengeance on Santa Claus moooaa ha ha ha! The raccoons will strike on midday December twenty-fifth this year since it will be on xmas DAY!".

" Retribution?" Sanford asked Comet, "Why does Sashi desire revenge?".

Comet took a deep breath after that discussed, "Santa put Sashi on the naughty list when she was a little raccoon.".

After that Sanford said, "Oh sibling.".

" Is it true or is she simply crazy?" I asked.

Sanford sat silently for a moment. I might tell he was assuming.

Finally, he asked, "Hey, exists anyhow that you know of to send a signal to one of the various other reindeers? In some way to let them know where you are?".

Comet slanted his head sideways as well as idea for a moment. "Well, there is a monitoring tool on my collar. Santa will certainly realize I am missing ultimately as well as will certainly find me. Yet it could be too late by that time.".

" Hmmm ..." I said. I wished to be extra handy. I was attempting to think. of a good concern to ask Comet as well.

" Hmmmm ..." stated Sanford," I question ..." He really did not complete his sentence; instead he went to consider Comet's collar. Sanford took a look at the red collar with silver bells. There was little blinking yellow light with a little black switch. "Hey, why is that light blinking and also what's with the switch?".

I got on top of Comet to obtain a closer look. "Possibly Santa is searching for you currently.".

Comet seemed to liven up. "You can be right. Can you push the black button that Sanford was speaking about? I never ever recognized it existed.".

" Sure." I pushed the switch, the light stopped flashing as well as ... nothing occurred. I looked at Sanford, waiting on him to say something. He really did not state anything. He was assuming, though.

" Hmmmm ..." was all that appeared of him.

Secs later, though, there was a knock on our door. "What the ... I claimed. Our workplace remained in a secret city, in a secret location. Nobody simply casually knocked on our door! It had not been also a door. Sanford looked at me. He was wishing I recognized who maybe at our door. Lastly Sanford simply shrugged and also responded to the door.

" Rex!" Comet said loudly. Comet was unexpectedly pleasant. Sanford and also I stared at the elf standing in our entrance ... He disappeared than three feet tall. He had red hair, pointy ears and a little round nose. His eyes were intense eco-friendly. He put on a white long sleeve t-shirt, red trousers as well as eco-friendly velour vest.

There was a huge reindeer standing right behind the elf. The reindeer was even larger than Comet.

Comet practically galloped to the door. "I concerned obtain Comet," the elf said in a deep New york city accent. "Santa could not press any type of charges if you hand him over now.".

I was stunned.

Sanford asked, "Why do you have a New york city accent?" The elf looked at us as if we were crazy.

" Look, I really did not come below to say. I got ta obtain Comet back to the North Post before Santa understands he's gone." Rex opened the door wider and entered our workplace with the other reindeer.

" Prancer?" Comet asked.

" Yes, it' me," Prancer stated, perturbed. "We need to come back. No more venturing off.

Wait a min. You said Santa was going to press fees," Sanford mentioned.Rex crossed his arms. His ears turned redder than his red hair, "No you are mistaken. I stated we obtained ta get Comet back prior to Santa presses charges. There's a difference, alright?" Rex started to speak faster as well as with panic in his voice, "Look, let me discuss something. Santa doesn't understand he is gone yet, all right? I can't simply return to the North Post without Comet. I am THE delay elf. I are accountable for the reindeer. Me. Me alone. Nobody else. Just me." Rex's hands were moving around as he talked. He started to pace backward and forward. "Rudolph currently charged me of not loading his water bucket. Rudolph is always charging me of something. Comet ..." Rex quit pacing as well as turned quickly to look at Comet.

"Allow's go. Prepare yourself to fly. We are going house in light speed, all right? No sluggish poking, sluggish moving. La la ligagging, okay? In fact, I'm going to ride you to see to it we obtain you house. No stopping for Egg Nog. You obtained it?"

Rex was kind of harsh as well as challenging. He got on top of Comet and also dug the heels of his sharp eco-friendly shoes right into Comet's side. "Let's go. Thank you for dealing with him as well as pushing the locator switch. If you had not pushed the switch I most likely wouldn't have found him till after Christmas." Comet walked outside with Rex on this back and also Prancer followed.

" However ..." both Sanford and I tried to clarify Comet's not flying conditions.

Rex held his hands up. "Don't worry. You will be considerably rewarded on Christmas from Santa, okay?" Rex checked out Prancer. "Let's go."

Prancer ran past Comet as well as promptly took off in trip. We might see him for just a couple of secs and after that he was entered a flash of light. Hey, ah ... Comet ..." Rex cleared his throat, "why are we still here?"

" The reason we are still here is because Sashi put a spell as well as I shed my flying powers."

Rex was still resting on Comets back, "However that does not make any sense. If you shed your powers, just how were you able to get right here?"

Comet clarified everything to Rex.

" You think Prancer will return for us?" Rex asked sadly. Comet reduced his head then trembled it. "No.".

Rex took a deep breath after that climbed up off his back.

Then Sanford stated, "Can not you simply push the switch on his collar once again?".

Rex smirked. "It's not that simple. For safety factors, we can just reply to the switch locator mechanism when every twelve hours.".

I drank my head. "That does not make any type of feeling.".

We had actually all been sitting in the office for an hour in silence. Rex consumed the last donut as well as consumed alcohol the last of the milk. He leaned back in his chair to massage his stomach from satisfaction. He leaned a little also much back because instantly his chair tilted back and then we heard of the large BOOM! Rex was laying level on his back. All that we can see were his environment-friendly elf footwear holding up airborne.
A minute later there was an additional unusual sound originating from the dumpster. It seemed like the first kernel standing out when making popcorn just louder. Sanford didn't intend to inform me to inspect it out this time. This moment he wasn't to inspect it out for himself. He jumped into the dumpster. The remainder of us stood outside the dumpster as well as waited on him to inform us what remained in there.

" Well?" I ultimately asked.
" Absolutely nothing. There is nothing in below." Then Sanford jumped out of the trash can. Equally as his paws will touch the ground they lifted up once more. The even more Sanford moved his legs about, the higher off the ground he went. "Woo hoo !!!" Sanford shouted in a cheer, "I'm flying! Me! I am ultimately flying!" He was ideal! He was flying! The problem was that he was too hectic overlooking at me with an I-told-you-so search in his eyes that he didn't see the wall surface until it was too late. Yep, he flew onto a wall surface and glided right down.
Rex was unexpectedly out of his unfortunate mood and right into an ecstatic as well as satisfied state of mind. He was raising and also down. "Oh, this is

terrific! This is definitely excellent!".

Comet on the other hand looked sadder than before. "Great," he said regretfully, "now he can fly but I still can't.".

Comet was about to turn around and also return right into the office yet Rex stopped him. "Comet, don't you see what occurred?".

Comet only shook his head to state no.

" Sanford has your powers. You were the one that was intended to jump into the dumpster just now, not Sanford. In some way your powers were placed on still setting and also kept in the dumpster. The noise that we listened to was your powers being renewed.".

" That does not make any type of sense," I claimed. I realized I seemed to be saying that a whole lot. Nothing regarding today made good sense.

Rex disregarded me as well as proceeded speaking to Comet. "We need to consider a way to redirect or transfer the powers from Sanford onto you.".

Sanford lastly sat up as well as drank his head. His ears waved every. which means as he did so. "I knew I can fly. I told you I could. That's why I constantly wore this cape. I understood I would need it someday.

I simply trembled my head in difference. Then I started to assume. I kept in mind a spell an old wizard buddy had taught me to redirect powers. I never ever believed I would in fact require to make use of the spell but this appeared to be a good time. "Rex, hello, I assume I might have a spell you can attempt.".

Rex considered me astonished and claimed, "A spell, from a computer mouse?".

I was angering. "I have some high friends in some high locations." Rex was silent.

" Do you wish to know the spell or otherwise? Or maybe I should cast the spell

on you?" I asked.
Rex's eyes grew large. He drank his head no and held his hand's up. "You go on and also do what you need to do.".
I looked at Sanford as well as stated, "Sanford, in order for the spell to function, you have to agree to give up your new discovered powers.".
Sanford's ears increased and also his head slanted sideways, "What?".
" You have to quit your powers. They aren't your own. You recognize that. They belong to Comet.".
Sanford appeared he intended to battle with me yet compelled himself to stand up to. Just as I was about to tell him the spell, a multi colored pet cat with black, white as well as orange patches of unbelievably long hair casually walked into our street. The feline hissed at me. "What the ...".

Rex sneezed and his nose turned an intense red. "Ah, guy, I dislike cats." He began making weird sounds with his throat.
" Oh no ..." Comet stated.
" What's wrong?" Sanford asked Comet. "That's Sashi's personal feline.".
I examined the cat as well as believed she looked a lot more like a instead of a personal aide.
" I heard that," she stated to me. I frowned, "Heard what?".
" I can review minds. I'm not a but my name is Luna.
The pet cat rested right before Comet and also Rex. "Yes," she said proudly, "I am Sashi's leading aide. Sashi desires all of you to report to the North Pole right away." She had a French accent.
I jumped onto Sanford's back. There was no other way I was mosting likely to be.

near to a cat who was proud to be the personal aide of an insane raccoon. Besides, her feline impulses might begin and she may follow me for no genuine reason.

" Why would certainly Sashi desire me to visit the North Post?" Sanford asked.

"She desires you powers ... duh.," the feline described.

" What does she desire with them?" I asked.

" You already recognize she intends to take over the North Pole. You are going to require to go to the North Post anyhow if you want to stop her.

I took a look at her suspiciously. I couldn't inform if she got on Sashi's side or Santa's side.

" She's right," Rex said. Sanford groaned.

" How are we going to obtain there?".

Luna waited. She walked to and fro near the dumpster and also began to purr.

"I have actually got it. All of you get involved in the dumpster," she required.

" Wait," Comet claimed, "Luna, just how did you obtain below?".

She grinned wickedly as well as her eyes glossed over. "I snuck into Santa's sleigh while the security fairies were doing a technique run of the sleigh. They found me in the rear seats and tossed me over the top. It turned out fine due to the fact that I only needed to walk a block to locate you." She removed her throat after that said, "Currently get into the dumpster, every one of you with the exception of Sanford.".

Rex led Comet to the dumpster. They both entered. I was a little disappointed given that they didn't argue. I thought they simply wanted to go.

home, however. I firmly insisted to remain on Sanford's back.

" Fine," Luna said checking out me. She read my mind once more. "You can stay on Sanford's back.".

Sanford ultimately talked, "What are we going do?".

" We need a rope to tie you to the dumpster to draw it as you fly." "What?!" Sanford as well as I heckled the exact same time.

Rex and Comet weren't phased whatsoever by the request. Comet nodded, "Yep, you have sufficient power to be able to draw all of us to the North Pole.".

Rex discovered a rope in the dumpster and also threw it bent on Luna. She discharged a happy, "Meow." Luna approached Sanford as well as swiftly linked the rope around his neck then hooked the various other end of the rope to the dumpster. Luna jumped into the dumpster after that said, "Now start running.".

Sanford looked fired up as well as began to run. I was worried that the rope would certainly snap or that Sanford would certainly not be strong enough to draw everyone and the dumpster yet to my surprise we were all soon in the air. Currently we just required to recognize the directions of just how to reach the North Post. Comet promptly shouted out, "Transform right! Obtain a little more rate or we will certainly all drop! Go greater and quicker!".

Sanford's tongue was now socializing as well as his paws were moving so quick I could not see them. We were over several planes and passed them up swiftly. A hr into the trip we encountered a snow storm. Comet shouted, "You need to get higher or we will certainly collapse! You need to obtain above the snow tornado!" Sanford did what he was told. Minutes later we saw a red blinking light on a pole.

" We're house!" Rex screamed excitedly and hugged Comet. Comet was grinning bright.

" Stop running or you'll pass up the North Post!" Luna shouted.

Sanford stopped running as well as we all started to drop. "Walk!!!" Comet shouted. "Walk slowly." As Sanford began a sluggish walk the autumn reduced to a soft glide. We lastly landed carefully on the snow. Sanford shed his balance and the dumpster toppled. A reindeer bounded over and also claimed, "Hey Comet. Hey Rex. Hey Luna ... Luna? Wait ... Luna, what are you doing here?" Prancer asked casually.

" I mobilized her," a high pitched squeaky voice said. Most of us turned to see a raccoon with a team of little animal close friends: there were a few.

penguins, a couple of cats, a few squirrels, a fox and more raccoons. Every one of them had gigantic ice in their hands. Sashi was in front and also in the middle of the pack. She had a mean and also cranky look on her face. "Comet, leave the dumpster. Prancer, remain where you are.".

" Much better do what she states ... she's not steady," Luna stated in her French.

accent.

Unexpectedly, Rex leapt out of the dumpster twirling with his toes pointed. As he landed, his appropriate foot promptly kicked Sashi right into the pond close by. The team of pets silenced for a moment, twirled about and their mouths dropped open, Sashi appeared of the water as well as drank her coat. She resembled a large hair ball.

The pets directed at Rex as well as shouted, "Charge!".

They threw the huge ice at Rex. He began escaping from them. Rex's eyes were broad from fright. I began to laugh from the view on his face and at exactly how amusing Sashi looked. That was when a penguin to throw an ice cube at me. I practically obtained crushed.

" Charlie," Sanford asked, "are you all right?".

Fortunately, it arrived at my tail. Sanford shoved the cube off of me. "I'm all right.".

Rex was running in circles and howling like a little woman. The pets lastly got so tired that they all practically laid down in the snow from fatigue.

Comet, Sanford as well as I walked over to where Sashi stood. She was quiet and she wasn't moving. We could not see her eyes. We might not see her hands, but we might see the Book of the North. An end of it was protruding of Sashi's hair. Sanford ordered it.

" Santa has a safety spell on guide. Guide should not ever splash or catch on fire. Whenever it is discovered swiped, the thief winds up iced up until guide is gone back to Santa," Comet clarified.

We left Sashi, Rex and the other pets and also took a trip to the village. I was delighted to go by Santa's workshop. I intended to go within yet Comet would not let us. He stated we needed to go see Santa right now.

We went to the largest residence. We walked in and also rose the stairways. Santa was being in a huge fuzzy red chair. There was a fire going in the massive stone fire area. Santa was using a white lengthy sleeve thermal tee shirt and also blue denim overalls. I thought he constantly used red or environment-friendly.

" Nope," Santa said, "I only wear my suit on Xmas day." "You check out minds, too?" I asked.

Santa nodded, "however only when they remain in the exact same area as me." He.

grinned.

Sanford gave Santa the Book of the North.

" Thank you," he said, "I will provide you added gifts at Xmas." Sanford and I both grinned large.

" Hey, I just thought of something," I stated, "Just how will we get Comet back to his old self?".

Santa looked at me. "Well, Charlie, you currently recognize the spell.

You're right; it is the one your close friend told you. However," he pointed at Sanford, "he needs to surrender the powers though.".

Sanford opened his mouth large. He drank his head as well as retreated.

" You had better state it now prior to he leaves the room," Santa advised me.

I depended on my back legs and also held my hands out towards Sanford after that claimed, "Hola hola hula hu hoop opposite and wadda loophole. There was a flash of light which filled the area. Santa and I covered our eyes. After a few secs the light lastly lowered. When I uncovered my eyes Sanford was putting down grumbling and also Comet was grinning.

" Well?" I asked.

" It worked," Sanford grunted unfortunately.

" Yippie!!!" Comet escaped and as quickly as he was outside he flew. away.

I was afraid to talk to Sanford. I understood he was mad at me. I had to do. what was right though.

Santa looked from Sanford to me and also back to Sanford. "Oh, I see." Sanford damaged at his chin. "Well, you can not fly however you can ride my sleigh anytime.".

Sanford appeared to liven up some. "Really?" "Actually," Santa claimed.

From then on every Christmas Santa would select us up and we would assist provide presents in our community. Oh, you're probably wondering what happened to Sashi. Santa let Rex select Sashi's penalty. Rex might have selected Sashi to be iced up every Christmas but for some crazy factor Rex pitied Sashi. So he chose Sashi would assist show ballet to several of the fairies. Sashi begged to be frozen rather.

Completion.

www.ingramcontent.com/pod-product-compliance
Lightning Source LLC
LaVergne TN
LVHW040942150826
845672LV00008B/2495

* 9 7 9 8 7 6 0 2 1 0 8 5 2 *